ARIZONA BEER

BREWING UNDER THE SUN

THE ULTIMATE GUIDE TO ARIZONA BREWERIES

Farabee Publishing

Farabee Publishing
P O Box 322
Chandler, Arizona 85244

Illustrations were contributed from many resources.
Thank you to everyone for your contributions to make the book possible.

ISBN: 978-1-942846-23-9

Library of Congress Number: 2016908996

Printed in the United States of America

THE ULTIMATE EXPERIENCE FOR BEER ENTHUSIASTS

Great Arizona Beer Tours has created the ultimate experience for Beer Enthusiasts.

You will be able to enjoy some of the finest craft brew Arizona has to offer.

Spend the day traveling around Arizona learning how they brew their Craft, sample some of their finest, and enjoy fine food.

You can design your own specialized tour and even cater it for 14, 20, or 27 of your closest friends on one of the comfortable mini-coaches.

Packages:

- One Day Beer Tour - 12 hours
- Two Day Beer Tour - 24 hours
- Create Your Own Tour
  You set the destination, breweries and round trip time.

CALL (602) 616-9866

www.GreatAZBeerTours.com

Info@GreatAZBeerTours.com

Thank you to everyone that contributed to the beginning and actual creating this book.

The purpose of the book is to promote Arizona Breweries. Arizona is rich in history, as portrayed in this book. We are also rich in entrepreneurship. This book only offers 90 Arizona Breweries. There are several we did not pick up. We will catch them on the next edition.

This book will provide everyone with the breweries in Arizona, their location and in some cases the beers they offer.

Visit a brewery near you or travel around the state to discover our rich heritage and have a beer along the way.

America now has more breweries than ever. And that might be a problem.

Fritz Hahn - 01/18/2016 - Washington Post

It was a startling announcement: As of Dec. 1, 2015, the Brewers Association had counted 4,144 breweries in the United States, the most ever operating simultaneously in the history of the country. According to historians, the previous high-water mark of 4,131 was set in 1873.

The new number includes giant Budweiser, artisan Dogfish Head and your neighborhood brewpub. Although beer industry observers have known this day was coming, the pace of growth was explosive: At the end of 2011, there were 2,033 breweries, or fewer than half as many as now. In 2005, there were only 1,447. And 25 years ago? The Brewers Association, a trade group for small and independent breweries, logged a mere 284 in 1990.

Table of Contents

Arizona Breweries in Alphabetical Order

8-Bit Brewing Co.
1050 Fairway Dr #101,
Avondale (623) 925-1650

Arizona Wilderness
Brewing Co.
721 N. Arizona Avenue,
#103, Gilbert

Bad Water Brewing Co
4216 N. Brown, Scottsdale
(480) 748-4460

Barley Brothers Brewery
1425 McCulloch Blvd
North, Lake Havasu City
(928) 505-7837

Barnstar Brewing Co
P. O. Box 60, Skull Valley
(928) 442-2337

Barrio Brewing Co.
800 East 16th Street,
Tucson (520) 791- 2739)

Beast Brewing Co.
1326 W. Highway 92, #8,
Bisbee (520) 284-5251

Beaver Street Brewery
11 S. Beaver Street,
Flagstaff (928) 779-0079

Birreria Italia
15444 N. Greenway
Hayden Loop
Scottsdale (480) 607-6458

BJ'S Restaurant & Brewery
- Chandler
3155 W. Chandler Blvd,
Chandler (480) 917-0631

BJ'S Restaurant & Brewery
- Desert Ridge
21001 N. Tatum
Boulevard, Phoenix
(480) 538-0555

BJ'S Restaurant & Brewery
6622 E. Superstition
Springs Blvd, Mesa
(480) 324-1675

BJ'S Restaurant & Brewery –
9748 W. Northern Ave,
Peoria (623) 772-6470

BJ'S Restaurant & Brewery –
4270 N. Oracle Road,
Tucson (520) 690-1900

BJ'S Restaurant & Brewery -
Tucson - Broadway
5510 E. Broadway Road,
Tucson (520) 512-0330

Black Bridge Brewing
421 E. Beale Street, Kingman
(928) 377-3618

Black Hole Beer Co.
1590 Swenson Street,
Prescott (928) 237-9029

Black Horse Brewery
1058 Burton Road
Show Low (928) 537-9349

Blasted Barley Beer Co
404 S. Mill Ave. Ste 101
Tempe (480)-967-5887

Borderlands Brewing Co.
119 E. Toole Avenue,
Tucson (520) 261-8773

Casa Arriba Brewing Co.
15025 N 74th St, Scottsdale
(480) 948-9969

Catalina Brewing Co.
P.O. Box 9038
Catalina (520) 329-3622

College Street Brewhouse &
Pub
1940 College Drive, Lake
Havasu City
(928) 854-2739

Corbett Brewing Company
414 N. 5th Avenue
Tucson   (520)770-1600

Desert Eagle Brewing Co.
150 Main Street, Mesa
(480) 656-2662

Dragoon Brewing Co.
1859 W. Grant Road, #111,
Tucson (520) 329-3606

Dubina Brewing Co.
17035 N 67th Ave #6,
Glendale
(623) 412-7770

El Viejon Brewing Company
1001 N 43 Rd Ave Lot 266,
Phoenix (480) 399-4133

Fate Brewing Co.
7337 E. Shea Blvd Suite 105
Scottsdale (480) 994 - 1275

Goldwater Brewing Co.
3608 N. Scottsdale Rd.
Scottsdale (480) 350-7305

Gordon Biersch Brewery
Restaurant - Tempe
420 S. Mill Avenue, Ste 201,
Tempe (480) 736-0033

Goldwater Brewing Co.
3608 N. Scottsdale Rd.
Scottsdale, AZ 85251

Gordon Biersch Brewery
Restaurant - Tempe
420 S. Mill Avenue, Suite
201, Tempe (480) 736-0033

Gordon Biersch Brewery
Restaurant – San Tan
2218 E. Williams Field Road,
Gilbert

Gordon Biersch Brewery
18545 N. Allied Way
Phoenix

Flagstaff Brewing Co.
16 East Route 66, Flagstaff
(928) 773-1442

Four Peaks Brewery - Grill & Tap
15745 N. Hayden Road, Scottsdale

Four Peaks Brewery - Sky Harbor
Terminal 4 3400 E. Sky Harbor Boulevard
Phoenix

Four Peaks Brewery - Tap Room
2401 S. Wilson Street
Tempe

Four Peaks Brewing Co.
1340 E. 8th Street, Tempe
(480) 303-9967

Freak'N Brewing Co.
9299 W. Olive Avenue, Suite 513, Peoria
(623) 738-5804

Gordon Biersch Brewery Restaurant - Westgate
6915 N. 95th Ave, Glendale

Grand Ave Brewing Co.
1205 W. Pierce Street, Phoenix (602) 670-5465

Grand Canyon Brewery
233 W. Route 66, Williams (800) 513-2072

Granite Mountain Brewing
123 N. Cortez Street, Prescott (928) 778-5535

Helton Brewing
2144 E. Indian School Rd, Phoenix (602) 730-2739

Historic Brewing Company
4366 E. Huntington Dr, #A, Flagstaff
(855) 484- 4677

Huss Brewing Co.
1520 W. Mineral Road, Suite 102, Tempe (480) 264-7611

Indigenous Aleworks
5752 E. Garnet Avenue
Mesa

Iron John's Brewing Co
245 S. Plumer Avenue, #27, Tucson   (520) 775-1727

Lonesome Valley Brewing
3040 N. Windsong Drive, #101 Prescott Valley
(928) 515-3541/ (602) 758-8336

Lost Dutchman Beer Co.
22620 S. 178th Place
Gilbert

Lumberyard Brewing Co.
5 S. San Francisco Street
Flagstaff   (928) 779-2739

Mad Cactus Brewery
3514 Kings Court Drive
Sierra Vista

Mesquite River Brewing
13610 N. Scottsdale Road, Suite 18, Scottsdale (602) 692-1920 (Opening 2016)

Mother Bunch Brewing
825 N 7th Street   Phoenix
(602) 368-3580

Mother Road Brewing Co.
7 South Mikes Pike, Flagstaff
(928) 774-9139

Mudshark Brewery
210 Swanson Avenue, Lake Havasu
(928) 453-2981

Nimbus Brewing Co.
3850 E. 44th Street, Tucson
(520) 745-9175

North Mountain Brewing Co.
522 E. Dunlap Avenue, Phoenix   602-861-5999

O.H.S.O Eatery + nano-Brewery
4900 E. Indian School Road, Phoenix (602) 955-0358

Oak Creek Brewery at Tlaquepaque
336 Highway 179, Sedona
(928) 203-9441

Oak Creek Brewing Co.
2050 Yavapai Drive, Sedona
(928) 204-1300

Oggi's Pizza & Brewing
6681 W Beardsley Rd, Glendale
(623) 566-8080

Old Bisbee Brewing Co.
200 Review Alley, Bisbee
(520) 432-BREW (2739)

Old World Brewery
334 N. 25th Avenue, Phoenix (623) 581-3359

Owl's Orchard Brewery
20518 E. Orchard Lane, Queen Creek, (480) 254-4070

Papago Brewing Co.
7107 E. McDowell Road, Scottsdale (480) 425-7439

Pedal Haus Brewery
730 S Mill Ave #102
Tempe (480) 314-2337

Peoria Artisan Brewery
10144 W Lake Pleasant Pkwy
Peoria (623) 572-2816

Peoria Artisan Brewery
107 W. Honeysuckle Street
Litchfield Park
(623) 536-4804

Phoenix Ale Brewery
3002 E. Washington Street, Phoenix (602) 275-5049

Pinetop Brewing Company
159 W. White Mountain Blvd
Pinetop-Lakeside
(928) 358-1971

Prescott Brewing Co.
130 W. Gurley Street, Suite A, Prescott
(928) 771-2795

Prison Hill Brewing Co.
278 S. Main Street, Yuma
(928) 276-4001

Pueblo Vida Brewing Co
115 E. Broadway Blvd,
Tucson (520) 623-7168

Rock Bottom Brewery &
Restaurant - Arrowhead
7640 W. Bell Road,
Glendale (623) 878-8822

Saddle Mountain Brewing
Company
15651 W. Roosevelt St.
Goodyear (623) 249-5520

San Tan Brewing Co.
8 S. San Marcos Place,
Chandler (480) 917-8700

Scottsdale Beer Company
8608 E Shea Blvd,
Scottsdale, (480) 219-1844

Sentinel Peak Brewing Co.
4746 E. Grant Road,
Tucson (520) 429-0244

Sleepy Dog Saloon &
Brewery
1920 E. University Drive,
#104, Tempe
(480) 967-5476

Superstition Meadery
120 W Gurley Street
Prescott (480) 296-3571

Ten Fifty-Five Brewing Co.
3810 E. 44th Street, Tucson
(520) 461-8073

THAT Brewery -
Cottonwood
300 E Cherry St,
Cottonwood

THAT Brewery Pine
3270 N. Highway 87, Pine
(928) 476-3349

The Address Brewing (1702)
1702 East Speedway Blvd,
Tucson (520) 325-1702

The Beer Research Institute
1641 S. Stapley Road, Suite
#105 Mesa (480) 892-2020

Sonoran Brewing Co.
3002 E. Washington Street,
Phoenix (602) 510-8996

SunUp Brewing Co.
322 E. Camelback Road,
Phoenix (602) 279-8909

The Perch Pub & Brewery
232 & 236 S. Wall Street
Chandler   (480) 773-7688

Thunder Canyon Brewery
7401 N. La Cholla Blvd,
Tucson (520) 797-2652

Thunder Canyon Brewery -
Downtown
220 E. Broadway Boulevard,
Tucson (520) 396.3480

Two Brothers Tap House
and Brewery Scottsdale
4321 N Scottsdale Rd,
Scottsdale (480) 378-3001

Uncle Bear's Brew House
Grill
4921 E. Ray Road, Suite B3,
Phoenix (480) 961-2374

Union Barrelhouse
3636 N. Scottsdale Rd,
Scottsdale (480) 946-7258

Verde Brewing Company
368 S. Main Street, Camp
Verde (928) 567-7033

Wanderlust Brewing Co
1519 N. Main Street, Ste 102
Flagstaff (928) 351-7952

Wren House Brewing Co
2125 N 24th St
Phoenix (602) 244-9184

Arizona Breweries by Location

Avondale/Goodyear

8-Bits Aleworks

1050 Fairway Dr
Building F - Suite 101
Avondale
http://www.8-bitbrewery.com/

Monday – Thursday: 4 pm – 9 pm
Friday: 3 pm – 9 pm
Saturday: 4 pm – 10 pm
Sunday: 12 pm – 8 pm
Tap Room

Goodyear

Saddle Mountain Brewing Company

15651 W. Roosevelt St.
Goodyear
http://www.goodyearaz.gov/

Sunday – Thursday: 11 am – 10 pm
Friday – Saturday: 11 am - 12 am

Restaurant Menu Available

Bisbee

Beast Brewing Co.

1326 W. Highway 92, #8
Bisbee
(520) 284-5251
http://www.beastbrewingcompany.com/

Monday – Thursday: Closed
Friday: 3 pm – 9 pm
Saturday: 12 pm – 9 pm
Sunday: 12 pm – 5 pm

Old Bisbee Brewing Co.

200 Review Alley
Bisbee
(520) 432-BREW (2739)
http://www.oldbisbeebrewingcompany.com/

Monday – Thursday,
Sunday: Noon – 10:30 pm
Friday – Saturday: Noon - 11:30 pm

Restaurant Selections

Camp Verde

Verde Brewing Company
368 S. Main Street
Camp Verde 86322
(928) 567-7033
www.verdebrewing.com

 **Verde Brewing Company**

Open daily from 11 am – 9 pm,
Friday & Saturday: 11 am - 10 pm

Restaurant Menu

Catalina

Catalina, Arizona, is perhaps the
nearest thing available these days to an
Old West boom town.

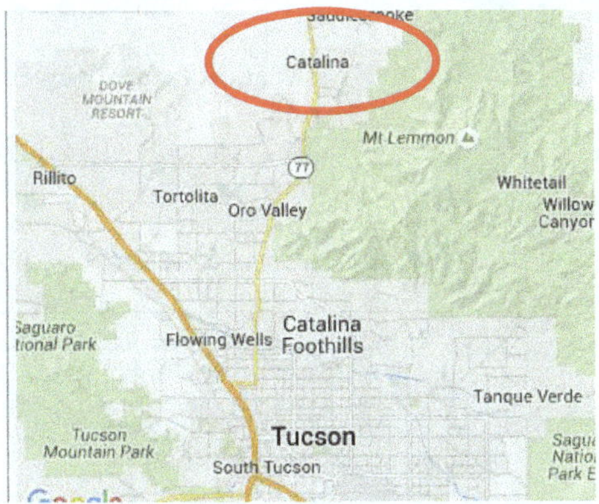

Catalina Brewing Co.
6918 N Camino Martin #120,
Catalina
http://www.catalinabrewingco.com/

Thursday: 4 pm - 9 p.m.
Friday: 4 pm - 10 p.m.
Saturday: Noon - 10 pm
Sunday: 11 am - 5 pm
Monday - Wednesday: Closed

Chandler

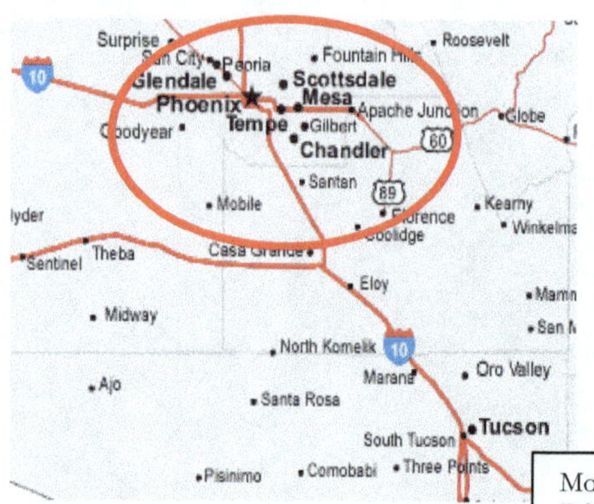

BJ'S Restaurant & Brewery - Chandler

3155 W. Chandler Boulevard
Chandler
(480) 917-0631
http://www.bjsrestaurants.com/

Monday - Thursday: 11:00 am - 12:00 am
Friday - Saturday: 11:00 am - 1:00 am
Sunday: 10:00 am - 11:00 pm

Restaurant Menu Available

SanTan Brewing Co.

8 S. San Marcos Place
Chandler 85225
(480) 917-8700
http://www.santanbrewing.com

The Perch Pub & Brewery

232 & 236 S. Wall Street
Chandler 85225
(480) 773-7688
http://perchpubbrewery.com/

San Tan Brewing Company Hours
Brewpub Hours
Sunday | 8 am – 11 pm
Monday-Thursday | 11 am – 11 pm
Friday + Saturday | 8 am – 1 am
Breakfast Hours
Friday-Sunday | 8 am – 10:45 pm
Lunch + Dinner Hours
Sunday-Thursday | 11 am – 10 pm
Friday + Saturday | 11 am – 12 am
Happy Hour
Monday-Friday | 3 pm – 6 pm
Reverse Happy Hour
Sunday-Thursday | 9 pm – Midnight

Restaurant Menu Available

Monday -Friday: 11 am - 1 am
Saturday -Sunday: 9 am - 1 am
Roof Top Open
Monday -Sunday: 4 pm - 1 am

Restaurant Menu Available

Flagstaff

Beaver Street Brewery

11 S. Beaver Street
Flagstaff
(928) 779-0079
http://www.beaverstreetbrewery.com/

Sunday – Thursday: 11 am -11 pm
Friday – Saturday: 11 am - 12 pm

Restaurant Menu Available

Flagstaff Brewing Co.

16 East Route 66
Flagstaff
(928) 773-1442
http://www.flagbrew.com/

11 am to 2 am Daily

Restaurant Menu Available

Historic Brewing Company

4366 E. Huntington Drive, #A
Flagstaff
(855) 484-HOPS (4677)

http://historicbrewingcompany.com/

Monday- Friday: 3 pm - 9 pm
Saturday - Sunday: 12 pm - 7 pm

Lumberyard Brewing Co.
5 S. San Francisco Street
Flagstaff
(928) 779-BREW (2739)
http://www.lumberyardbrewingcompany.com/

Mother Road Brewing Co.
7 South Mikes Pike
Flagstaff,
(928)-774-9139

Monday – Thursday: 2 pm - 9 pm
Friday – 2 pm – 10 pm
Saturday: Noon - 10 pm
Sunday Noon – 9 pm

Restaurant Menu Available

Wanderlust Brewing Co.
1519 N. Main Street, Suite 102
Flagstaff
(928) 351-7952
http://www.wanderlustbrewing.com/

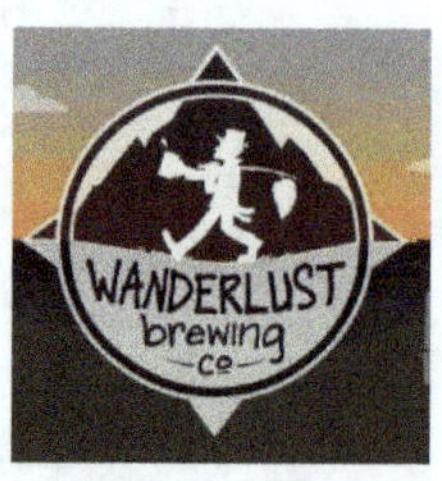

Monday-Thursday: 2 pm - 9 pm
Friday: 2 pm-10 pm
Saturday: Noon-10 pm
Sunday: Noon-9 pm

Gilbert

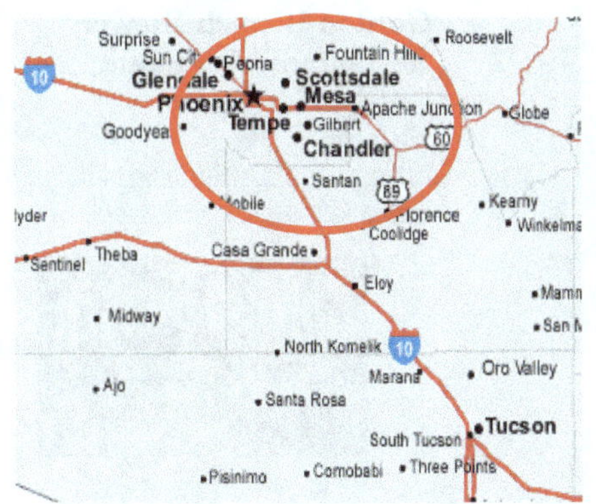

Arizona Wilderness Brewing Co.

721 N. Arizona Avenue, #103
Gilbert
(480)284-9863
http://www.azwbeer.com/

Monday-Thursday: 11 am - 11 pm
Friday -Saturday: 11 am - 1 am
Sunday: 11 am - 10 pm

Restaurant Menu Available

Gordon Biersch Brewery Restaurant - SanTan

2218 E. Williams Field Road
Gilbert
http://www.gordonbiersch.com/

Sunday – Wednesday: 11 am - 11 pm
Thursday: 11 am - 12 am
Friday - Saturday: 11 am - 1 am

Restaurant Menu Available

Glendale

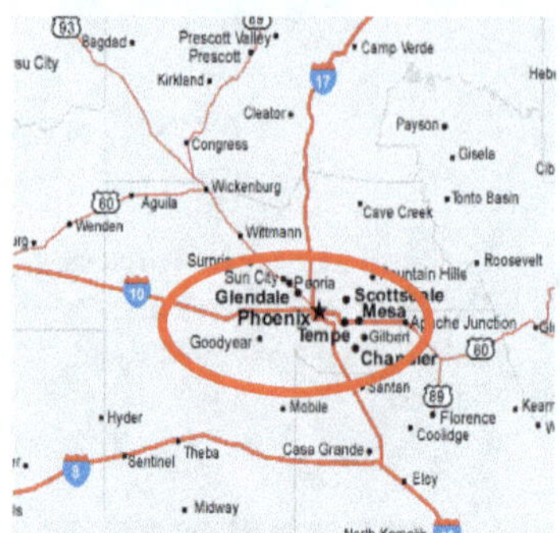

Dubina Brewing Co.

17035 N 67th Ave #6,
Glendale
(623) 412-7770
http://www.dubinabrewing.com/

Tuesday -Thursday: 3 pm – 10 pm
Friday: 3 pm – 12 am
Saturday: 11 am – 12 am
Sunday: 11 am – 9 pm

Restaurant Menu Available

Gordon Biersch Brewery Restaurant - Westgate

6915 N. 95th Avenue
Glendale
http://www.gordonbiersch.com/locations/glendale?action=view

Sunday -Wednesday: 11 am - 11 pm
Thursday: 11 am - 12 am
Friday - Saturday: 11 am - 1 am

Restaurant Menu Available

Rock Bottom Brewery & Restaurant - Arrowhead

7640 W. Bell Road
Glendale
(623) 878-8822
http://www.rockbottom.com/locations/arrowhead

Rock Bottom Brewery
Sunday -Wednesday: 11 am - 12 am
Thursday: 11 am - 1 am
Friday - Saturday: 11 am - 1 am

Restaurant Menu Available

Kingman

Wicked Poison

Raspberry Poison

Wicked Ginger

Black Bridge Brewing
421 E. Beale Street
Kingman
(928) 377-3618
http://www.blackbridgebrewery.com/

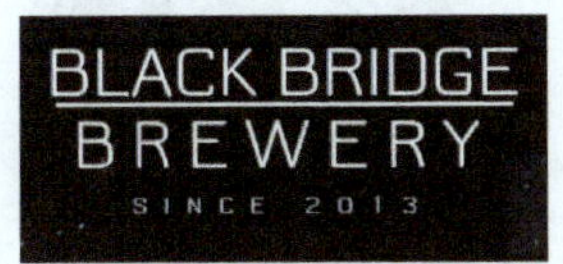

Black Bridge Brewing
Tuesday -Wednesday: 11 am - 9 pm
Thursday - Saturday: 11 am - 11 pm
Sunday: 10 am - 4 pm
Closed Mondays

Lake Havasu

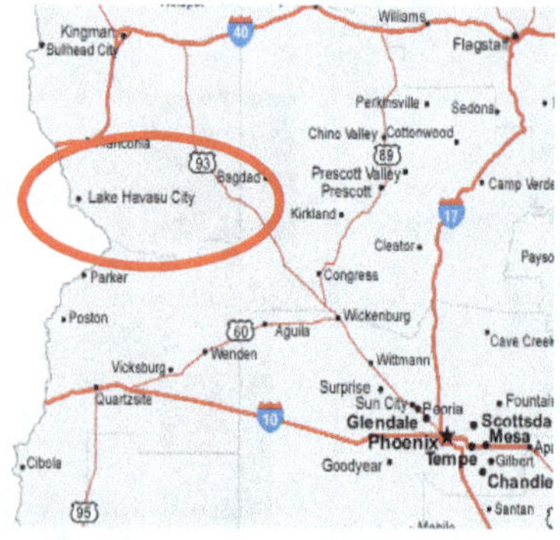

Barley Brothers Brewery
1425 McCulloch Boulevard North
Lake Havasu City
(928) 505-7837
http://barleybrothers.com/

College Street Brewhouse & Pub
1940 College Drive
Lake Havasu City
(928) 854-2739
http://www.collegestreetbrewhousean
dpub.com/

Sunday -Thursday: 11 am - 9 pm
Friday - Saturday: 11 am - 10 pm

Restaurant Menu Available

Sunday -Thursday: 11 am - 9 pm
Friday - Saturday: 11 am - 10 pm

Restaurant Menu Available

Mesa

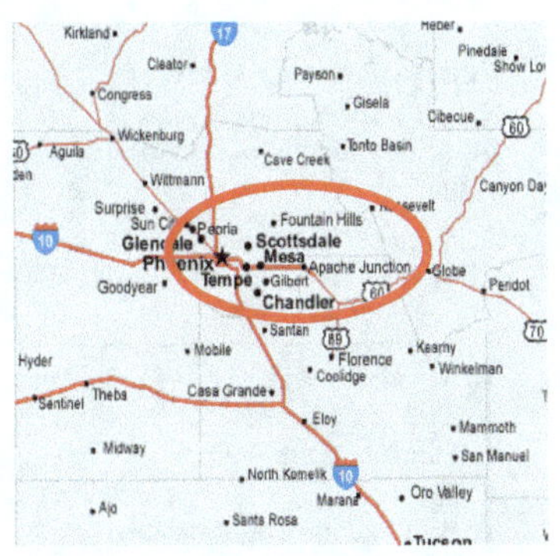

BJ'S Restaurant & Brewery - Mesa

6622 E. Superstition Springs Boulevard
Mesa
(480) 324-1675
http://www.bjsrestaurants.com/locati
ons/az/mesa

Monday-Thursday: 11 am-12 am
Friday: 11 am-1 am
Saturday: 10 am-1 am
Sunday: 10 am-11 pm

Restaurant Menu Available

Desert Eagle Brewing Co.

150 Main Street
Mesa
(480) 656-2662
http://deserteaglebrewing.com/

Monday 3 pm – 10 pm
Tuesday – Friday 3 pm -12 am
Saturday 11 am – 12 am
Sunday: - 11 am -9 pm

Restaurant Menu Available

The Beer Research Institute

1641 S. Stapley Road, Suite #105
Mesa
(480) 892-2020
http://www.thebeerresearchinstitute.c
om/

Monday – Wednesday, 11 am -10 pm
Sunday: - 11 am -10 pm
Thursday – Saturday: 11 am - 12 am

Restaurant Menu Available

Peoria

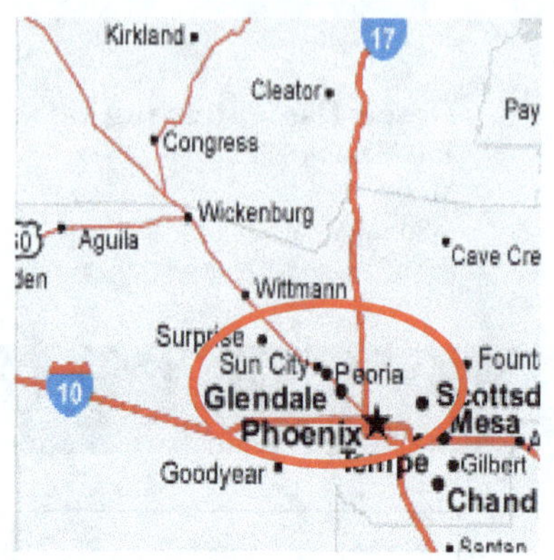

BJ'S Restaurant & Brewery - Peoria

9748 W. Northern Avenue
Peoria
(623) 772-6470
http://www.bjsrestaurants.com/locations/az/peoria

Freak'N Brewing Co.

9299 W. Olive Avenue, Suite 513
Peoria
(623) 738-5804
http://freaknbrew.com/

Thursday & Friday: 3 pm – 8 pm
Saturday: 2 pm - 8 pm
Sunday: 2 pm – 6 pm

Peoria Artisan Brewery

North Peoria Brewery
10144 W Lake Pleasant Pkwy, Peoria AZ 85383
(623) 572-2816
http://www.peoriaartisanbrewing.com/

Monday-Wednesday: 11 am - 9 pm,
Thursday-Saturday: 11 am - 10 pm,
Sunday: 10 am – 9 pm

Restaurant Menu Available

Peoria Artisan Brewery

(formerly the Arrogant Brewer)
107 W. Honeysuckle Street
Litchfield Park
(623) 536-4804
http://www.peoriaartisanbrewing.com

Tuesday – Thursday: 3 pm – 10 pm
Friday - Saturday: 12 – 10 pm
Sunday Noon – 8 pm
Closed Mondays

Phoenix

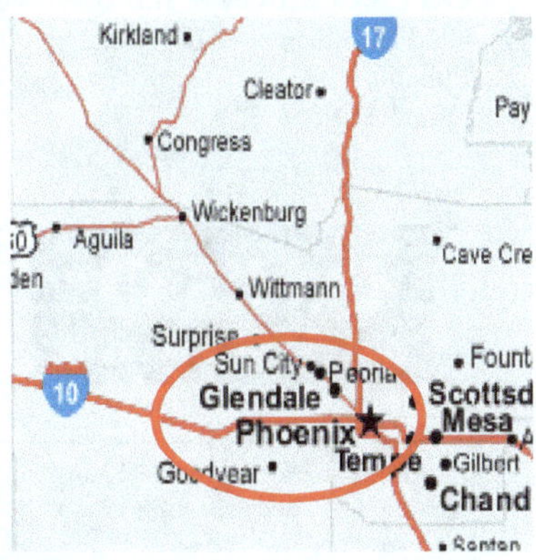

BJ'S Restaurant & Brewery - Desert Ridge

21001 N. Tatum Boulevard
Phoenix
(480) 538-0555
http://www.bjsrestaurants.com/locati
ons/az/desert-ridge

Monday-Thursday: 11 am – 12 am
Friday: 11 am – 1 am
Saturday: 10 am – 1 am
Sunday: 10 am – 11 pm

Restaurant Menu Available

Four Peaks Brewery - Sky Harbor

Terminal 4 3400 E. Sky Harbor
Boulevard
Phoenix
http://www.fourpeaks.com/our-
pubs/#

Gordon Biersch Brewery Restaurant - Scottsdale

18545 N. Allied Way
Phoenix
http://www.gordonbiersch.com/locati
ons/scottsdale?action=view

Grand Avenue Brewing Co.

1205 W. Pierce Street
Phoenix
https://www.facebook.com/GrandAv
enueBrewingCompany

Helton Brewing

2144 E. Indian School Rd
Phoenix
http://heltonbrewing.com/

Tuesday – Thursday: 3 pm – 9 pm
Friday: 3 pm – 10 pm
Saturday: Noon – 10 pm
Sunday: Noon – 7 pm
Closed Mondays

Cheese and Charcuterie

Mother Brunch Brewing
825 N 7th Street
Phoenix
(602) 368-3580
http://www.MotherBunchBrew.com

Monday – Thursday: 11 am – 10 pm
Friday: 11 am – 12 am
Saturday: 10 am – 12 am
Sunday: 10 am – 10 pm

Restaurant Menu Available

North Mountain Brewing Co.
522 E. Dunlap Avenue
Phoenix
(602) 861-5999
http://www.northmountainbrewing.com/

Monday – Wednesday 3 pm – 10 pm
Thursday: 11 am – 10 pm
Friday & Saturday: 11 am – 11 pm
Sunday: 11 am – 9 pm

Restaurant Menu Available

O.H.S.O Eatery + nanoBrewery
4900 E. Indian School Road
Phoenix
(602) 955-0358
http://ohsobrewery.com/

Monday – Friday: 11 am – 12 am
Saturday – Sunday: 9 am – 12 am

Restaurant Menu Available

Phoenix Ale Brewery
3002 E. Washington Street
Phoenix
http://www.phoenixbrew.com/

Monday – Saturday: Noon – 7 pm
Sunday: Noon – 6 pm

Restaurant Menu Available

Sonoran Brewing Co.

3002 E. Washington Street
Phoenix
(602) 510-8996
http://www.sonoranbrewing.com/

SunUp Brewing Co.

322 E. Camelback Road
Phoenix
(602) 279.8909
http://www.sunupbrewing.com/

Sunday– Thursday 11 am – 11 pm
Friday - Saturday 11 am – 12 am

Restaurant Menu Available

Uncle Bears Brewery

4921 E Ray Rd, Phoenix
(480) 961-2374
http://ubbrewery.com/

Uncle Bear's Brewery
Sunday – Thursday: 11 am – 11 pm
Friday - Saturday: 11 am – 1 am

Restaurant Menu Available

Wren House Brewing Company

2125 N 24th St
Phoenix
(602) 244-9184
http://wrenhousebrewing.com/

Monday – Thursday: 3 pm – 9 pm
Friday – Saturday: 12 pm – 10 pm
Sunday: Noon – 7 pm

Pine/ Pinetop-Lakeside/Show Low

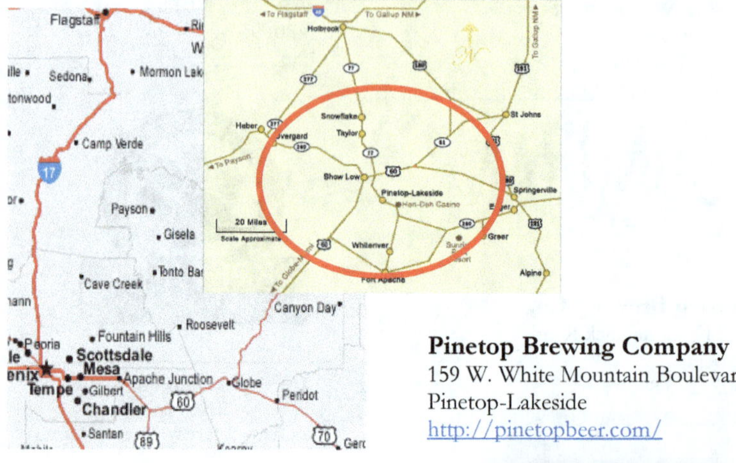

Pinetop Brewing Company
159 W. White Mountain Boulevard
Pinetop-Lakeside
http://pinetopbeer.com/

THAT Brewery
3270 N. Highway 87
Pine
(928) 476-3349
http://www.thatbrewery.com/

Sunday - Thursday: 11 am – 8 pm
Friday – Saturday: 11 am –10 pm
Sunday: 11 am – 8 pm

Sunday, Monday, Wednesday,
Thursday: 11 am – 8 pm
Friday – Saturday: 11 am – 9 pm
Sunday: Noon – 6 pm

Restaurant Menu Available

Black Horse Brewery
1058 Burton Road
Show Low
(928) 537 -9349
blackhorsebrewery@gmail.com

Thursday – Sat:
Noon– 8 pm
Sun: Noon – 5 pm

Prescott

Black Hole Beer Co.
1590 Swenson Street
Prescott
(928) 237-9029
http://www.blackholebeercompany.com/

Prescott Brewing Co.
130 W. Gurley Street, Suite A
Prescott
(928) 771-2795
http://www.prescottbrewingcompany.com/

11 am – 10 pm daily Restaurant Menu Available

Lonesome Valley Brewing
3040 N. Windsong Drive, #101
Prescott Valley
(928) 515-3541/ (602) 758-8336
http://www.lonesomevalleybrewing.com/

Monday – Thursday: 11 am – 8 pm Friday – Saturday: 11 am – 10 pm Sunday: 11 am – 5 pm Restaurant Menu Available

Granite Mountain Brewing
123 N. Cortez Street
Prescott
http://granitemountainbrewing.com/

Wednesday, Thursday: 4 pm – 9 pm Friday: 4 pm – 10 pm Saturday: 11 am – 10 pm Sunday: 1 pm – 6 pm

Scottsdale

Bad Water Brewing Company

4216 N. Brown
Scottsdale
(480) 748-4460
www.badwaterbrewing.com

Tuesday- Thursday: -4 pm – 10 pm
Friday – Saturday: 11 am – 11 pm
Sunday: 4 pm – 10 pm

Restaurant Menu Available

Fate Brewing Co.

7337 E. Shea Boulevard, Suite 105
Scottsdale
(480) 994-1275
http://www.fatebrewing.com/

Monday – Thursday: -3 pm – 10 pm
Friday – Saturday: 11 am – 11 pm
Sunday: 11 am – 9 pm

Restaurant Menu Available

Four Peaks Brewery - Grill & Tap

15745 N. Hayden Road
Scottsdale
https://www.facebook.com/fourpeaks
north?fref=ts

Papago Brewing Co.

7107 E. McDowell Road
Scottsdale
(480) 425-7439
http://papagobrewing.com/

Sunday – Thursday: Noon - Midnight
Friday – Saturday: Noon – 2 am

Restaurant Menu Available

Two Brothers Tap House and Brewery Scottsdale
4321 N Scottsdale Rd,
Scottsdale
(480) 378-3001

http://www.twobrothersbrewing.com

/scottsdale/

Monday – Thursday: 11 am – 10 pm
Friday – Saturday: 11 am – 11 pm
Sunday: 11 am – 9 pm

Restaurant Menu Available

Union Barrelhouse
3636 N. Scottsdale Rd,
Scottsdale
(480) 946-7258
http://unionbarrelhouse.com/

Monday – Thursday: 11 am – 12 am
Friday: 11 am – 2 am
Saturday: 10 am – 2 am
Sunday: 10 am – 12 am
Restaurant Menu Available

Scottsdale Beer Company

8608 E Shea Blvd
Scottsdale,
(480) 219-1844
http://www.scottsdalebeercompany.com/

Monday – Thursday: 11 am – 10 pm
Friday – Saturday: 11 am – 11 pm
Sunday: 11 am – 9 pm

Restaurant Menu Available

Goldwater Brewing Co.
3608 N. Scottsdale Rd.
Scottsdale
http://www.goldwaterbrewing.com/#craft-beer-brewery

Monday – Thursday: 3 pm – 10 pm
Friday: 1 pm – 12 am
Saturday: 11 am – 12 am
Sunday: 1 pm – 8 pm

Sedona

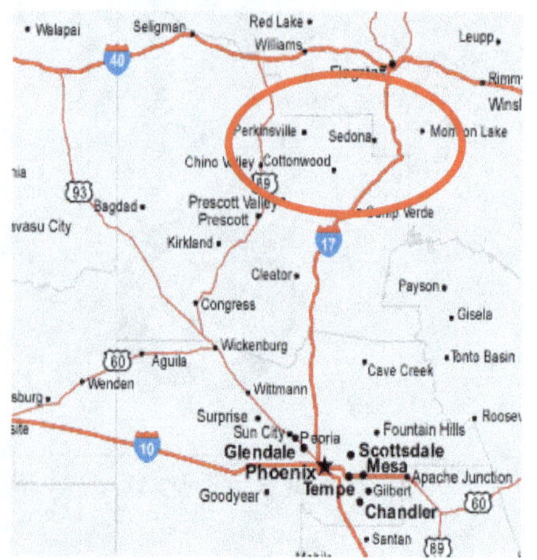

Oak Creek Brewing Co.
2050 Yavapai Drive
Sedona
(928) 204-1300
http://www.oakcreekbrew.com/

12 Noon to close
Restaurant Menu Available

Oak Creek Brewery at Tlaquepaque
336 Highway 179
Sedona
(928) 203-9441
http://www.oakcreekpub.com

Serving 11:30 am – 8:30 pm

Restaurant Menu Available

THAT Brewery - Cottonwood
300 E Cherry St,
Cottonwood,
http://thatbrewery.com/cottonwood/

Monday - Thursday: 4 pm – 8 pm
Friday 2 pm – 9 pm
Saturday: Noon – 9 pm
Sunday: Noon – 7 pm

Skull Valley

BarnStar Brewing Company
4050 N. Tonto Road
(Forest service Rd. 102, Prescott National Forest)
Skull Valley, Arizona 86338
(928) 442-2337
http://www.barnstarbrew.com/

We hope you will join us on a Saturday or Sunday between 12:00-5:00.

Tempe

Blasted Barley Beer Co

404 S. Mill Ave. Ste 101
Tempe
(480)-967-5887
http://blastedbarley.com/

Cartel Brewery

225 W University Drive, #103
Tempe, AZ 85281
http://www.cartelbrewery.com/welcome/

Tuesday – Friday: 3 pm – 10 pm
Saturday: Noon – 10 pm
Sunday – Noon – 8 pm

Tap Room

The Shop – Opening September 2016
922 W. 1st Street,
Tempe (602) 717-4237

Cartel Brewery moving to a new Tap Room

Blasted Barley Beer Co.
Monday -Wednesday: 11 am – 12 am
Friday: 11 am – 2 am
Saturday: 10 am – 2 am
Sunday – 10 am – 12 am
Sat/Sun Brunch 10:30 am – 3 pm

Restaurant Menu Available

Four Peaks Brewery - Tap Room

2401 S. Wilson Street
Tempe
http://www.fourpeaks.com/

Friday: 4 pm – 9 pm

Tasting Room

Four Peaks Brewing Co.

1340 E. 8th Street
Tempe
(480) 303-9967
http://www.fourpeaks.com/

Sunday – Thursday: 11 am – 11 pm
Friday – Saturday: 11 am – 2 am
Sunday: 10 am – 1 am

Restaurant Menu Available

Gordon Biersch Brewery Restaurant – Mill Ave

420 S. Mill Avenue, Suite 201
Tempe
480-736-0033
http://www.gordonbiersch.com/

Sunday – Wednesday: 11 am – 11 pm
Thursday: 11 am – 12 am
Friday – Saturday: 11 am – 1 am

Restaurant Menu Available

Huss Brewing Co.

1520 W. Mineral Road,
Suite 102
Tempe
(480) 264-7611
http://hussbrewing.com/

Pedal Haus Brewery

730 S Mill Ave #H102
Tempe
http://www.pedalhausbrewery.com/

Sunday – Wednesday: 11 am – 11 pm
Thursday: 11 am – 12 am
Friday - Saturday: 11 am – 1 am

Restaurant Menu Available

Sleepy Dog Saloon & Brewery

1920 E. University Drive, #104
Tempe
(480) 967-5476
http://sleepydogbrewing.com/

Tuesday – Friday: 4 pm – 11 pm
Saturday: 2 pm – 12 am
Sunday - Monday Closed

Light Menu Available

Huss Brewing Co.
Monday – Thursday: -3 pm – 8 pm
Friday: – 3 pm – 10 pm
Saturday: Noon – 10 pm
Sunday: 11 am – 2 pm

Restaurant Menu Available

Tucson

Barrio Brewing Co.

800 East 16th Street
Tucson
(520) 791-BREW (2739)
http://www.barriobrewing.com/

Monday – Wednesday: 11 am – 10 pm
Thursday – Saturday: 11 am – 12 am
Sunday: 11 am – 9 pm

Restaurant Menu Available

BJ'S Restaurant & Brewery - Tucson

4270 N. Oracle Road
Tucson
(520) 690-1900
http://www.bjsrestaurants.com/locations/az/tucson

Monday – Thursday: 11 am – 12 am
Friday: 11 am – 1 am
Saturday: 10 am – 1 am
Sunday: 10 am – 12 am
Restaurant Menu Available

BJ'S Restaurant & Brewery –

Tucson - Broadway
5510 E. Broadway Road
Tucson
(520) 512-0330
http://www.bjsrestaurants.com/

Monday – Thursday: 11 am – 12 am
Friday: 11 am – 1 am
Saturday: 10 am – 1 am
Sunday: 10 am – 12 am
Restaurant Menu Available

Borderlands Brewing Co.

119 E. Toole Avenue
Tucson
(520) 261-8773
http://borderlandsbrewing.com/

Wednesday – Thursday: Noon – 9 pm
Friday – Saturday: Noon – 10 pm
Sunday: Noon – 5 pm

Dragoon Brewing Co.
1859 W. Grant Road, #111
Tucson
(520) 329-3606
http://www.dragoonbrewing.com/

Wednesday – Friday: 3 pm – 10 pm
Saturday: Noon – 10 pm
Sunday: Noon – 5 pm

Iron John's Brewing Company
245 S. Plumer Avenue, #27
Tucson
(520) 775-1727

http://www.ironjohnsbrewing.com

Monday – Saturday: 11 am – 7 pm
Closed on Sunday

Nimbus Brewing Co.
3850 E. 44th Street
Tucson
(520) 745-9175
http://www.nimbusbeer.com/

Monday – Thursday: 11 am – 11 pm
Friday - Saturday: 11 am – 1 am
Sunday: 11 am – 9 pm

Restaurant Menu Available

Pueblo Vida Brewing Co
115 E. Broadway Boulevard
Tucson
http://www.pueblovidabrewing.com/

Monday – Thursday: 4 pm – 10 pm
Friday: Noon – 12 am
Saturday: Noon – 12 am
Sunday: Noon – 6 pm

Sentinel Peak Brewing Co.

4746 E. Grant Road
Tucson
Taylor Carter
(520) 429-0244
http://www.sentinelpeakbrewing.com/

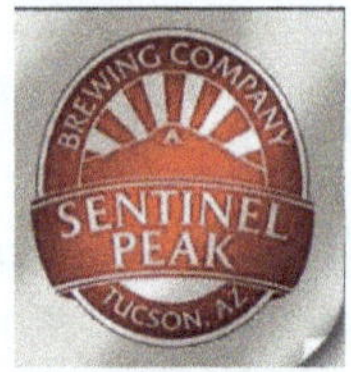

Tuesday – Thursday: 11 am – 9 pm
Friday - Saturday: 11 am – 10:30 pm
Sunday: 11 am –8 pm

Restaurant Menu Available

Ten Fifty-Five Brewing Co.

3810 E. 44th Street
Tucson
(520) 461-8073
http://1055brewing.com/

Thursday – Friday: 4 pm – 8 pm
Saturday: 2 pm – 7 pm

The Address Brewing (1702)

1702 East Speedway Blvd
Tucson
(520) 325-1702
http://www.1702az.com/

Monday – Friday: 11 am – 11 pm
Saturday: Noon – 11 pm
Sunday: Noon – 10 pm

Restaurant Menu Available

Thunder Canyon Brewery

7401 N. La Cholla Boulevard
Tucson
(520) 797-2652
http://thundercanyonbrewery.com/

Thunder Canyon Brewery -

220 E. Broadway Boulevard
Tucson
(520) 396-3480
http://thundercanyonbrewery.com/

Monday – Sunday 11 am – 11 pm

Restaurant Menu Available

Williams

Grand Canyon Brewery

233 W. Route 66
Williams
(800) 513-2072
http://www.grandcanyonbrewery.com/

All of our beer is served and sold at our conjoining restaurant Cruisers Cafe 66, located directly in front of the brewery. Tours are given upon request, please speak with someone at the restaurant.

11:00 am – 11:00 pm 7 days a week

Yuma

Prison Hill Brewing Co.

278 S. Main Street
Yuma
(928) 276-4001
http://www.prisonhillbrewing.com/

Sunday – Thursday: 11 am – 10 pm
Friday – Saturday: 11 am – 2 am

Restaurant Menu Available

Purchase Arizona Craft Beer

Chandler

BevMo!
Wine Store
Wine, beer & spirits superstore
7230 W Ray Rd
Chandler, AZ
(480) 961-9100
Open until 9:00 PM

Cold Beers & Cheeseburgers
1980 W Germann Rd
(480) 899-2007
Open until 12:00 AM

Hungry Monk, Chandler
1760 W. Chandler Blvd
Chandler, AZ 85224
Between Pennington and Dobson on Chandler Blvd
www.hungrymonkaz.com

Total Wine & More
Wine Store
Wine, liquor & beer specialist
8544 S Emerald Dr.
Tempe, ·AZ
(480) 753-4225
Open until 10:00 PM

Whole Foods Market (Chandler)
2955 W Ray Rd.,
Chandler, AZ 85224

Gilbert

Fox Cigar Bar
1464 E Williams Field Rd #105,
Gilbert, AZ 85295

House of Brews
Cooper Marketplace
825 S Cooper Rd
Gilbert, AZ
(480) 426-9787

Total Wine and More
2224 E Williams Field Rd.,
Gilbert, AZ 85295

World of Beer, Gilbert
2224 E. Williams Field, Suite 107
Gilbert, AZ 85295
*1 Block West of the 2020 on E. Williams Field
Road in Gilbert* www.WorldOfBeer.com

Glendale

BevMo - Growler Stations
6712 W Bell Rd.,
Glendale, AZ 85308

Old Chicago
5695 W Bell Rd
Glendale, AZ
(602) 938-8808
Open until 2:00 AM

Goodyear

Caballero Grill
1800 N Litchfield Rd.,
Goodyear, AZ 85395

Litchfield Park

Ground Control
4860 N Litchfield Rd
Litchfield Park, AZ
(623) 535-9066
Open until 10:00 PM

Mesa

Sun Devil Liquors
235 N Country Club Dr.
Mesa, AZ
(480) 834-5050

The Brass Tap
Mesa Riverview
1033 N Dobson Rd #104
(480) 610-2337
Open until 12:00 AM

Phoenix

Arcadia Premium
5618 E Thomas Rd. #100,
Phoenix, AZ 85018

Angels Trumpet Ale House
810 N 2nd St
Phoenix, AZ
(602) 252-2630
Open until 12:00 AM

Central Kitchen
5813 N. 7th Street #140
Phoenix, AZ 85014
(602) 313-8705

Half Moon Sports Grill,
Biltmore Location
2121 E. Highland Avenue
Phoenix, AZ 85016
20th Street and Highland in Phoenix.
www.halfmoonsportsgrill.com

Hillside Spot Cafe
4740 E Warner Rd.,
Phoenix, AZ 85044

Pane Bianco
4404 N Central Ave.,
Phoenix, AZ 85012

The Little Woody
4228 E Indian School Rd.,
Phoenix, AZ 85018

Total Wine & More
Wine, liquor & beer specialist
1670 E Camelback Rd
Phoenix, AZ
(602) 279-0540
Open until 10:00 PM

Whole Foods Market (Scottsdale)
7111 E Mayo Blvd.,
Phoenix, AZ 85054

Scottsdale

BevMo - Growler Stations
7129 E Shea Blvd.,
Scottsdale, AZ 85254

BevMo - Growler Stations
7129 E Shea Blvd.,
Scottsdale, AZ 85254

Cactus Food Mart
8040 E Thomas Rd
Scottsdale, AZ
(480) 947-8886
Open until 11:00 PM

Cartel Coffee Lab - Scottsdale
7124 E. 5th Ave, Scottsdale
(480) 621-6381

Cold Beers & Cheeseburgers
4222 N Scottsdale Rd
Scottsdale, AZ
(480) 941-2747

Cold Beers & Cheeseburgers
20831 N Scottsdale Rd #117
Scottsdale, AZ
(480) 513-2747
Open until 10:00 PM

Craft 64
6922 E. Main Street
Scottsdale, AZ 85251
Located in Old Town Scottsdale on Main Street just west of Scottsdale Road.
www.craft64.com

Hopdoddy Burger Bar
11055 N Scottsdale Rd
Scottsdale, AZ
(480) 348-2337
Open until 10:00 PM

Sip Coffee & Beer House
3617 N Goldwater Blvd
(480) 625-3878
Open until 9:00 PM

Scottsdale Beer Company
8608 E Shea Blvd
Scottsdale, AZ
(480) 219-1844
Open until 11:00 PM

The Western
6830 E 5th Ave.,
Scottsdale, AZ 85251

Yard House
Scottsdale Fashion Square
7014 E Camelback Rd #612
Scottsdale, AZ
(480) 675-9273
Open until 11:00 PM

Sedona

Vino Di Sedona
2575 AZ-89A
Sedona, AZ

Tempe

BevMo - Growler Stations
15 S McClintock Dr.,
Tempe, AZ 85281

Cartel Coffee Lab - Tempe
225 W. University Drive, Tempe
(480) 621-6381

Eclectic Cafe
8544 S Emerald Dr.,
Tempe, AZ 85284

Flanny's Bar & Grill
1805 E. Elliott Rd.,
Tempe, AZ 85284

Mellow Mushroom, Tempe
740 S. Mill Ave, D100
Tempe, AZ 85281
On Mill Avenue in Downtown Tempe
www.mellowmushroom.com

Spokes on Southern
1470 E Southern Ave.,
Tempe, AZ 85282

The Handlebar Tempe
680 S Mill Ave
Tempe, AZ
(480) 474-4888
Open until 2:00 AM

Tilted Kilt Tempe
660 Warner Rd
Tempe, AZ
(480) 592-0102
Open until 12:00 AM

Tops Liquors
403 W University Dr #104
Tempe, AZ
(480) 967-5643
Open until 12:00 AM

World of Beer, Tempe
526 S. Mill Ave
Tempe, AZ 85281
*Located on Mill Avenue and 6th Street in
Downtown Tempe*
www.WorldOfBeer.com

Yucca Tap Room
29 W. Southern Ave.,
Tempe, AZ 85282

Tucson

**Best Western Royal Inn &
Suites –**
1015 N Stone Ave.,
Tucson, AZ 85705

Casa Video
Growler Fills
2905 E Speedway Blvd,
Tucson, AZ 85716

Cartel Coffee Lab - Tucson
2516 N. Campbell Ave, Tucson
(480) 621-6381

Casino Del Sol
5655 W Valencia Rd,
Tucson, AZ 85757

Driftwood Bar and Lounge –
Permanent Handle
2001 S. Craycroft Rd.,
Tucson, AZ 85711

Dry River Pizza Company
800 N Kolb Road,
Tucson, AZ 85710

Eclectic Cafe
7053 E Tanque Verde Rd,
Tucson, AZ 85715
Phoenix Area Locations
Flagstaff Locations

El Charro Downtown –
(Noche Dulce)
311 N Court Ave,
Tucson, AZ 85701

Mr. Head's Art Gallery and Bar
513 N 4th Ave,
Tucson, AZ 85705

Pastiche Modern Eatery –
3025 N Campbell Ave.,
Tucson, AZ 85719

Proper
(La Morena)
 300 E Congress Street,
Tucson, AZ 85701

Risky Business
250 S Craycroft Rd.,
Tucson, AZ 85711

SoSoBa – Citrana
12 E Route 66 #104
Flagstaff, AZ 86001

Tap & Bottle –

Cans, Rotating Handle & Growler Station
403 N 6th Ave.,
Tucson, AZ 85701

The Conspiracy Food Co-op
Growler Station
412 N 4th Ave,
Tucson, AZ 85705

Union Public House-
4340 N Campbell Ave #103,
Tucson, AZ 85718

Whole Foods – Bar 77
7133 N Oracle Rd,
Tucson, AZ 85704

Whole Foods
5555 E River Rd. #151,
Tucson, AZ 85750

Williams

South Rims Wine & Beer Garage
514 E Rte. 66
Williams, AZ
(928) 635-5902
Open until 9:00 PM

Crescent Crown Distributors

1640 W. Broadway Road
Mesa, AZ 85202-1117
(480) 685-2000

13430 W. Sweetwater Ave.
Surprise, AZ 85379-4273
(480) 685-2000
http://az.crescentcrown.com

DISTRIBUTOR OF THE WORLD'S
FINEST BEVERAGES
http://az.crescentcrown.com/events/
for events and lots of fun drinking your
favorite beer.

Distributes these Local Arizona Beers

Beer and Wine Distributors of Arizona

40 N. Central, Suite 1400
Phoenix, AZ 85004
http://www.bwdaz.com/

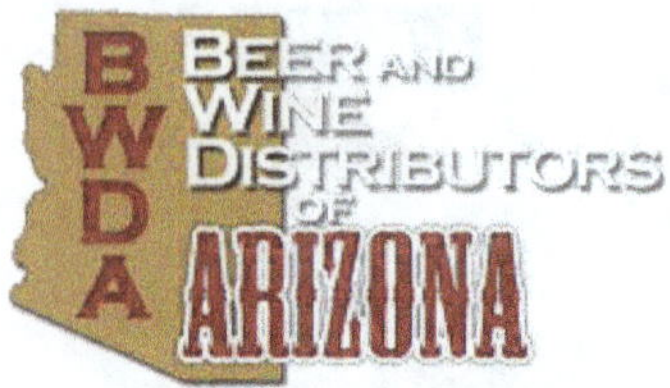

The Shop Beer
Company

Hensley Beverage Company

4201 N. 45th Ave. Phoenix, AZ 85031
Main: 602.264.1635
Customer Service: 602.264.1635 ext. 7212
http://hensley.com/

Barrio Brewing

Four Peaks
Brewing

Lumberyard
Brewing

Mother Road
Brewing

Mudshark
Brewery

Oak Creek
Brewing

Prescott
Brewing

Arizona Beer & Cider

http://azbeercider.com/

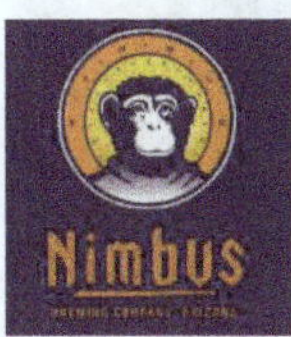

Romer Beverage Company

2908 E Andy Devine Ave
Kingman, Arizona 86401
http://www.romerbeverage.com/

Mudshark
Arizona, Craft Beer

Sleepy Dog Brewery
Arizona, Craft Beer

Four Peaks Brewery
Arizona, Craft Beer

Prescott Brewing
Arizona, Craft Beer

Mother Road Brewing
Arizona, Craft Beer

Arizona Beer Events

These are a few of the Events that happen around Arizona every year.

Arizona Strong Beer Festival™
February 10th, 2018
Steele Indian School Park in Phoenix.

Made in the Shade
June 9th 2018
1:00 pm - 5:00 pm
Pepsi Amphitheater –
Ft. Tuthill County Park,
Flagstaff AZ 86001
https://beerfests.com/

The Great American Barbecue & Beer Festival
March 24th 2018
3 S Arizona Ave. Chandler, AZ 85225

Mile High Brewfest
Saturday, August 11, 2018
4:00 pm - 8:00 pm
Prescott Mile High Middle School Field
 300 S Granite St., Prescott, AZ 86303
http://www.milehighbrewfest.com/

Baja Beer Festival
April 2018
Rillito Park. Tucson. 4-9 pm
Join our Celebration of Craft Beer with over 50 breweries and over 200 craft beers on tap.

32nd Annual Great Tucson Beer Festival Date to be Announced
Kino Sports North Complex, located at 2817 E Ajo Way, Tucson
6-10 pm
http://azbeer.com/tucson.htm

Real Wild & Woody
Date to be Announced
2:00 pm - 6:00 pm
Phoenix Convention Center –
100 N 3rd St.,
Phoenix AZ 85004
https://beerfests.com/

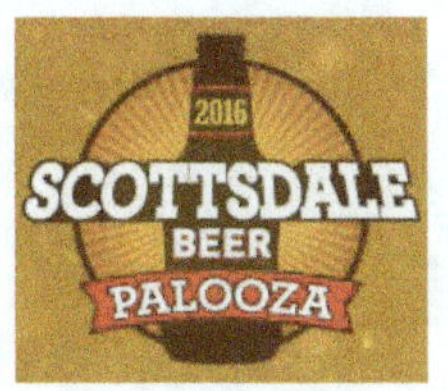

Scottsdale Beer Palooza
Date to be Determined
1:00 pm - 6:00 pm
WestWorld of Scottsdale –
16601 N. Pima Rd,
Scottsdale AZ 85260
https://beerfests.com/

The Great American Beer Fest
Date to be Announced
Check with http://azbeer.com/
Moved to Downtown Phoenix

www.ingramcontent.com/pod-product-compliance
Lightning Source LLC
Chambersburg PA
CBHW061101050726
47592CB00004B/1773